Loving Jesus, Died for Me

The story of our salvation for children, based on Matthew 26:26–30, 36–56; 28:1–10; and Luke 22:3–22, 39–53

Written by Naomi Moon
Illustrated by David Miles

CONCORDIA PUBLISHING HOUSE · SAINT LOUIS

Jesus Christ came down to be
God's pure Son, who sets us free.
He loves us eternally.
Loving Jesus, died for me.

It is passed, this wine and bread.
His body given; His blood shed,
Poured out for many, Christ said.
Loving Jesus, died for me.

Jesus prayed, eyes filled with tears.
Troubled, with so much to bear,
Yet He knew God's will was clear.
Loving Jesus, died for me.

Judas's heart was turned away.
He betrayed Christ and went astray;
Rejected God for what man paid.
Loving Jesus, died for me.

It is finished; His head bowed.
The sky turned dark and filled with clouds.
The curtain tore—now there's no doubt.
Loving Jesus, died for me.

Then the women sought to share
News that Jesus' tomb was bare.
The Lord's body was not there.
Loving Jesus, rose for me.

Christ appeared with words of peace
For the world, the great and least.
Spread this news to all you meet.
Loving Jesus, rose for me.

He will return for me and you,
And everything will be made new—
Restored, forgiven, renewed.
Loving Jesus, lives for me.

Dear Parent,

Just days earlier, followers of Jesus had rejoiced as He made His way into the city. During those happy (final) days, they heard Him preach and witnessed His miracles. Then, they lost Him. Their innocent Teacher was ridiculed, tortured, and killed in a horrifying, brutal act. The Roman spear that pierced Jesus' side proved He was dead.

Then, He wasn't.

What words describe how the disciples and other followers felt that morning? Stunned. Awed. Incredulous. Baffled. Language is inadequate. Human understanding is inadequate. But the truth is that Jesus was dead and is now alive.

This book refers to events of Holy Week and Easter to emphasize that Jesus lived and died and rose for us. As true God, He knew what would happen. As true man, He experienced physical suffering and death. And as our Redeemer and Savior, He gives Himself wholly to earn forgiveness for us. His love is personal and specific—for each of us.

As you read this book with your little one, have him or her repeat the last line of each verse with you to reinforce the message that Jesus lived, died, rose, and saves us. We can be confident that Jesus will return and that those who know Him as the Savior will be with Him forever.

He is risen! He is risen, indeed!

The Editor